TEMPTATION

by

DIETRICH BONHOEFFER

SCM PRESS LTD
56 BLOOMSBURY STREET
LONDON

VERSUCHUNG
edited by Eberhard Bethge,
first published by Chr. Kaiser Verlag,
Munich, 1953

English translation by Kathleen Downham
First published 1955
Reprinted 1956
Reprinted 1959
Reprinted 1961
Reprinted 1963
Reprinted 1964

Made and printed by offset in Great Britain by
William Clowes and Sons, Limited, London and Beccles

CONTENTS

I. LEAD US NOT INTO TEMPTATION 9
Preliminary
Abandonment
The Occasion
A Bond

II. THE TWO TEMPTATION STORIES 14
ADAM
CHRIST
The Temptation of the Flesh
Spiritual Temptation
Complete Temptation

III. THE TEMPTATION OF CHRIST IN HIS PEOPLE 22
THE TAKING OVER OF THE TEMPTATIONS
THE THREE AUTHORS OF TEMPTATION
The Devil
Lust
God himself

IV. CONCRETE TEMPTATIONS AND THEIR CONQUEST 31
THE TEMPTATIONS OF THE FLESH
Desire
Suffering
General Suffering
Suffering for Christ's sake
THE TEMPTATIONS OF THE SPIRIT
Securitas
Desperatio
THE LAST TEMPTATION

V. THE LEGITIMATE STRUGGLE 46

NOTE

From April 12-17, 1937, there was a reunion of the clergy who two years earlier, under the leadership of Dietrich Bonhoeffer, had established the seminary of the Confessing Church in Finkelwalde, near Stettin, and had finished the first course. Dietrich Bonhoeffer introduced each day with a Bible study on Temptation. The manuscript survived, and needed only to be put in order.

E. B.

I

LEAD US NOT INTO TEMPTATION

PRELIMINARY

Abandonment

LEAD us not into temptation. Natural man and moral man cannot understand this prayer. Natural man wants to prove his strength in adventure, in struggle, in encounter with the enemy. That is life. 'If you do not stake your life you will never win it.' Only the life which has run the risk of death is life which has been won. That is what natural man knows. Moral man also knows that his knowledge is true and convincing only when it is tried out and proved, he knows that the good can live only from evil, and that it would not be good but for evil. So moral man calls out evil, his daily prayer is—Lead me into temptation, that I may test out the power of the good in me.

If temptation were really what natural man and moral man understand by it, namely, testing of their own strength—whether their vital or their moral or even their Christian strength—in resistance, on the enemy, then it is true that Christ's prayer would be incomprehensible. For that life is won only from death and the good only from the evil is a piece of thoroughly worldly knowledge which is not strange to the Christian. But all this has nothing to do with the temptation of which Christ speaks. It simply does not touch the reality which is meant here. The temptation of which the whole Bible speaks does not have to do with the testing of my strength, for it is of the very essence of temptation in the Bible that all my strength—to my horror, and without my being able to do anything about it—is turned against me; really all my powers, including my good and pious powers (the strength of my faith), fall into the hands of the enemy power and are now led into the field against me. Before there can be any testing of my powers, I have been robbed of them. 'My heart trembles, my strength has left me, and the light of my eyes has departed from me' (Ps. 38.10). This is the decisive fact in the temptation of the Christian, that he is *abandoned*, abandoned by all his powers—indeed, attacked by them—abandoned by all men, abandoned by God himself. His heart shakes, and has fallen into complete darkness. He himself is nothing. The enemy is everything. God has 'taken his hand away from him' (*Augsburg Confession*, XIX), 'He has left him for a little while' (Isa. 54.7). The man is alone in his temptation. Nothing stands by him. For a little while the devil has room. How is the abandoned man to face the devil? How can he protect himself? It is the prince of this world who opposes him. The hour of the fall has come, the irrevocable, eternal fall: for who will free us again from the clutches of Satan?

A defeat shows the physical and the moral man that his powers have to increase before they can withstand the trial. So his defeat is never irrevocable. The Christian knows that in every hour of temptation all his strength will leave him. For him temptation means a dark hour which can be irrevocable. He does not seek for his strength to be proved, but he prays, 'Lead us not into temptation.' So the biblical meaning of temptation is not a testing of strength, but the loss of all strength, defenceless deliverance into Satan's hands.

The Occasion

Temptation is a concrete happening which juts out from the course of life. For the physical man all life is a struggle, and for the moral man every hour is a time of temptation. The Christian knows hours of temptation, which differ from hours of gracious care and preservation from temptation as the devil is different from God. The saying that every moment of life is a time of decision is for him a meaningless abstraction. The Christian cannot see his life as a series of principles, but only in its relation to the living God. The God who causes day and night to be gives also seasons of thirst and seasons of refreshment; he gives storms and peace, times of grief and fear, and times of joy. 'Weeping may tarry for the night, but joy cometh in the morning' (Ps. 30.5). 'To every thing there is a season, and a time to every purpose under the heaven: a time to be born, and a time to die; a time to plant, and a time to pluck up that which is planted; a time to kill, and a time to heal; a time to break down, and a time to build up; a time to weep, and a time to laugh . . . . He hath made every thing beautiful in its time' (Eccles. 3.1-4, 11). It is not what life may be in itself, but how God now deals with me, which matters for the Christian. God rejects me, and he accepts me again. He destroys my work, and he builds it up again. 'I am the Lord, and there is none else. I form the light, and create darkness; I make peace, and create evil' (Isa. 45.7).

So the Christian lives from the times of God, and not from his own idea of life. He does not say that he lives in constant temptation and constant testing, but in the time when he is preserved from temptation he prays that God may not let the time of temptation come over him.

Suddenly temptation comes upon the pious man.

'Suddenly do they shoot at him, and fear not' (Ps. 64.4) at a time when he least expected it. 'For man also knoweth not his time . . . even so are the sons of men snared in an evil time, when it falleth suddenly upon them' (Eccles. 9.12). 'For suddenly shall the wrath of the Lord come forth, and in thy security thou shalt be destroyed, and perish in the day of vengeance' (Ecclus. 5.7). So the Christian recognizes the cunning of Satan. Suddenly doubt has been sowed in his heart, suddenly everything is uncertain, what I do is so meaningless, suddenly sins of long ago are alive in me as though they had happened today, and they torture and torment me, suddenly my whole heart is full of deep sorrow for myself, for the world, for God's powerlessness over me, suddenly my vexation with life will lead me to terrible sin, suddenly evil desire is wakened, and suddenly the Cross is upon me and I tremble. This is the hour of temptation, of darkness, of defenceless deliverance into Satan's hands.

A Bond

But is the hour of temptation not bound to come? So is it not illegitimate to pray in this way? Ought we not rather to pray that in the hour of temptation, which is bound to come, strength may be given us to overcome our temptation? Such a thought claims to know more about temptation than Christ himself, and wants to be better than he who knew the hardest temptation. 'Is temptation not bound to come?' Then why? Must God deliver up his own to Satan? Must he lead them to the abyss where they fall? Must God yield such power to Satan? Who are we to speak of temptation being bound to come? Are we in God's counsel? And if—in virtue of a divine bond which is incomprehensible to us—temptation is bound to come, then Christ, the most tempted of all, summons us to pray against the divine bond—not to yield in stoic resignation to temptation, but to flee from that dark bond, in which God lets the devil do his will, and call to the open divine freedom in which God tramples the devil under foot. 'Lead us *not* into temptation.'

II

THE TWO TEMPTATION STORIES

AFTER these preliminary questions we must approach the point of the prayer 'Lead us not into temptation'. He who taught the disciples to pray in this way was Jesus Christ who alone must have known what temptation was. And because he knew he wanted his disciples to pray, 'Lead us not into temptation'. From the point of view of the temptation of Jesus Christ alone can we understand the meaning of temptation for us.

The Bible is not like a book of edification, telling us many stories of men's temptations and their overcoming. To be precise, the Bible tells only two temptation stories, the temptation of the first man and the temptation of Christ, that is the temptation which led to man's fall, and the temptation which led to Satan's fall. All other temptations in human history have to do with these two stories of temptation. Either we are tempted in Adam or we are tempted in Christ. Either the Adam in me is tempted—in which case we fall. Or the Christ in us is tempted—in which case Satan is bound to fall.

ADAM

The temptation of the first man presents the enigma of the tempter in paradise. We are very prone to look behind that happening over which the mystery of the unrevealed must lie, namely the origin of the tempter.

From that happening in paradise we learn three things.

First, that the tempter is to be found wherever there is innocence. Indeed the tempter is only to be found where there is innocence; for where there is guilt, he has already gained power.

Second, it is the quite unmediated appearance of the tempter in the voice of the serpent in paradise, the presence of Satan in paradise—in no way established or justified (not even by any philosophy about Lucifer)—which brings out his character as seducer. It is the same inscrutable, contingent suddenness of which we spoke before. The voice of the tempter does not come out of an abyss only recognized as 'Hell'. It completely conceals its origin. It is suddenly near me and speaks to me. In paradise it is the serpent—quite plainly a creature of God—through whom the tempter speaks to Eve. Indeed there is no sign of the origin of the tempter in fire and brimstone. The denial of the origin belongs to the essence of the seducer.

Third, in order, however, to win access to innocence, it is necessary that the denial of origin should be maintained until the end. Innocence means clinging to the Word of God with pure, undivided hearts. Thus the tempter must introduce himself in the name of God. He bears with him the Word of God and expounds it: 'Has God really said?' Have you understood God, the Lord, rightly here? Ought not another construction to be put on his Word? We cannot imagine the nameless dread which must have beset the first man in the face of such a possibility. In front of innocence yawns the abyss of yet unknown guilt; in front of faith the abyss of unknown doubts; in front of life the abyss of yet unknown death. This dread belonging to innocence, which the devil will rob of its only strength, the Word of God, is the sin of the seduction. It is not a question of engaging in a struggle, of the freedom of decision for good or for evil—it is not concerned with the ethical concept of seduction. Rather is Adam delivered up defenceless to the tempter. He lacks every insight, power, perception, which would have equipped him for the struggle with this adversary. He is left quite alone. The abyss has opened up beneath him. Only one thing remains: in the midst of this abyss he is upheld by the hand of God, by God's Word. Thus, in the hour of temptation, Adam can only shut his eyes and stand and let himself be upborne by the grace of God. But Adam falls. 'Has God really said?' In the abyss of this question Adam sinks and with him the whole of mankind. From the time of Adam's expulsion from paradise every man is born with this question, which Satan has put in Adam's heart. That is the first question of all flesh: 'Has God really said?' By this question all flesh comes to fall. The seduction of Adam brings all flesh to death and condemnation.

CHRIST

In the likeness of sinful flesh the Son of God, Jesus Christ our Saviour, came upon the earth. In him was all desire and all fear of the flesh, all damnation of the flesh and alienation from God. He 'hath been in all points tempted like as we are, yet without sin' (Heb. 4.15). If he was to help man, who is flesh, he had to take upon himself the whole temptation experience of the flesh. Even Jesus Christ κατὰ σάρκα was born with the question: 'Has God really said?'—yet without sin.

The temptation of Christ was harder, unspeakably harder, than the temptation of Adam; for Adam carried nothing in himself which could have given the tempter a claim and power over him. But Christ bore in himself the whole burden of the flesh, under the curse, under condemnation; and yet his temptation was henceforth to bring help and salvation to all flesh.

The Gospel reports that Jesus was led up of the Spirit into the wilderness to be tempted of the devil (Matt. 4.1). Therefore the temptation does not begin with the Father equipping the Son with every power and every weapon, in order that he might be victorious in the struggle; but the Spirit leads Jesus into the wilderness, into solitude, into abandonment. God takes from his Son all help of man and creature. The hour of temptation must find Jesus weak, lonely, and hungry. God leaves man alone in temptation. So Abraham had to be quite alone on the mountain in Moriah. Yes, God himself abandons man in face of temptation. Only thus can one understand II Chron. 32.31: 'God left Hezekiah to try him', or the Psalmists' repeated cry: 'God, forsake me not' (Ps. 38.21; 71.9, 18; 119.8). 'Hide not thy face from me; . . . . cast me not off, neither forsake me, O God of my salvation' (Ps. 27.9)—which must be incomprehensible to all human-ethical-religious thinking. God shows himself in temptation not as the gracious, the near one, who furnishes us with all the gifts of the Spirit; on the contrary he forsakes us, he is quite distant from us; we are in the wilderness. (Later we shall have more to say about this.)

In distinction from the temptation of Adam and all human temptations the tempter himself comes to Jesus (Matt. 4.3). Whereas elsewhere he makes use of creatures, here he himself must conduct the struggle. This makes it clear that in the temptation of Jesus it is a matter of the whole. It is here that the fullest denial of the origin of the tempter is to be found. It may be with reference to the denial of Satan's origin and the temptation of Jesus that Paul said: 'Even Satan fashioneth himself into an angel of light' (II Cor. 11.14). We should probably not think that Jesus did not recognize

Satan, but that Satan was so enticing that, in this way, he purposed to bring about the fall of Jesus.

The Temptation of the Flesh

Jesus has fasted forty days in the wilderness, and he is hungry. Then came the seducer to him. The tempter begins with the acknowledgement of Jesus as the Son of God. He does not say: 'Thou art the Son of God'—he cannot say that!—But he says: If thou art the Son of God, thou who sufferest hunger, command that these stones become bread. Here Satan tempts Jesus in the weakness of his human flesh. He wishes to set his Godhead against his manhood. He plans to make the flesh rebellious towards the spirit. Satan knows that the flesh is afraid of suffering. But why should the Son of God suffer in the flesh? The purpose of this question is clear. Were Jesus in the power of his Godhead to withdraw from suffering in the flesh, all flesh would be lost. The way of the Son of God on earth would be at an end. The flesh would once more belong to Satan. Jesus' answer with the Word of God shows, first of all, that even the Son of God stands under the Word of God, and that he can and will claim no individual right beside this Word. Secondly, it shows that Jesus will rely on this Word alone. The flesh, too, belongs to the Word of God, and if it must suffer, this means that man does not live by bread alone. Jesus has preserved his manhood and his way of suffering in temptation. The first temptation is the temptation of the flesh.

Spiritual Temptation

In the second temptation Satan begins as in the first: If thou art the Son of God—but he piles on his temptation by himself quoting God's Word against Jesus. Even Satan can use God's Word in the struggle. Jesus has to allow his Sonship to be attested. He is to demand a sign from God. That is the temptation of Jesus' faith, the temptation of the spirit. If the Son of God is to be in the midst of men's suffering, then ask for a sign of the power of God, which can save him at any time. Jesus' answer sets God's Word against God's Word, but in such a way that there is no fatal uncertainty, and so that truth is set against lies. Jesus calls this temptation a temptation of God. He will remain only by his Father's Word; that suffices him. If he had wanted more than this Word, he would have given place in himself to doubt in God. Faith which demands more than the Word of God in precept and promise, becomes a temptation of God. To tempt God means to lay upon God himself guilt, unfaithfulness and falsehood, instead of upon Satan. To tempt God is the highest spiritual temptation.

Complete Temptation

Satan comes differently the third time—without the declaration about the Sonship, without the Word of God. He comes now—and that is the decisive thing—in his wholly unconcealed display of power as the prince of this world. Now Satan fights with his very own weapons. There is no more veiling, no more dissimulation. Satan's power matches itself directly against the power of God. Satan hazards his ultimate resources. His gift is immeasurably big and beautiful and alluring; and in return for this gift he claims—worship. He demands open apostasy from God, whose only justification is the size and beauty of Satan's kingdom. This temptation shows with great clarity and insight completely final denial of God and submission to Satan. It is the temptation to the sin against the Holy Ghost.

Because Satan has fully revealed himself, he must be addressed, encountered and rejected by Jesus: 'Get thee hence Satan; for it is written, Thou shalt worship the Lord thy God, and him only shalt thou serve.'

Jesus is tempted in his flesh, in his faith and in his allegiance to God. All three are the one temptation—to separate Jesus from the Word of God. The nature of the flesh is used by Satan against the divine command. If Satan once gets power over the flesh of Jesus, Jesus will be in his hands. If Jesus will not rely on the Word alone, only believing, blindly believing and obeying, he is no longer the Christ and redeemer of men who can only find salvation through faith in the Word. So Satan has tempted the flesh and spirit of Jesus against the Word of God. The third temptation attacks the whole physical-spiritual existence of the Son of God. 'If thou dost not want to be inwardly torn by me, give me the whole of thyself—and I will make thee great in this world, in hatred of God and in power against him.' Thus Jesus suffers the temptation of the flesh, the high spiritual temptation, and, finally, the complete temptation, and in all three only the one temptation of the Word of God.

The temptation of Jesus is not that heroic struggle of man against wicked powers that we fondly and lightly suppose. In the temptation Jesus is robbed of all his own strength, he is left alone by God and man, in anguish he must suffer Satan's robbery, he has fallen into the deepest darkness. He is left with nothing but the saving, supporting, enduring Word of God, which holds him firmly and which fights and conquers for him. The night of the last words of Jesus—'My God, my God, why hast thou forsaken me'—has fallen, it must follow the hour of this temptation as the last fleshly-spiritual, complete temptation of the Saviour. The suffering by Jesus of abandonment by God and man is God's Word and judgement for him. In his defenceless, powerless submission to the power of Satan the reconciliation arises. He was tempted like as we are—yet without sin.

Thus, in the temptation of Jesus, there really remains nothing except God's Word and promise, no native strength and joy for the fight against wickedness, only God's strength and victory, which holds fast in the Word, and the Word robs Satan of his power. Only by God's Word is the temptation overcome.

'Then the devil leaveth him'. As in the beginning God had abandoned him, now the tempter abandons him—'and behold angels came and ministered unto him.' In the Garden of Gethsemane, too, 'there appeared unto him an angel from heaven, strengthening him' (Luke 22.43). That is the end of the temptation, that he who has entered into all weakness but who has been upheld by the Word, receives from an angel of God refreshment of all his powers of body, soul and spirit.

III

THE TEMPTATION OF CHRIST IN HIS PEOPLE

THE TAKING OVER OF THE TEMPTATIONS

BY the temptation of Jesus Christ the temptation of Adam is brought to an end. As in Adam's temptation all flesh fell, so in the temptation of Jesus Christ all flesh has been snatched away from the power of Satan. For Jesus Christ wore our flesh, he suffered our temptation, and he won the victory from it. Thus today we all wear the flesh which in Jesus Christ vanquished Satan. Both our flesh and we have conquered in the temptation of Jesus. Because Christ was tempted and overcame, we can pray: Lead us not into temptation. For the temptation has already come and been conquered. He did it in our stead. 'Look on the temptation of thy Son Jesus Christ and lead *us* not into temptation'. Of the granting of that prayer we may and should be certain; we should utter our amen to it, for it *is* granted in Jesus Christ himself. From henceforth *we* shall no longer be led into temptation, but every temptation which happens now is the temptation of Jesus Christ in his members, in his congregation. We are not tempted, *Jesus Christ is tempted in us.*

Because Satan could not bring about the fall of the Son of God, he pursues him now with all temptations in his members. But these last temptations are only the off-shoots of the temptation of Jesus on earth; for the power of temptation is broken in the temptation of Jesus. His disciples are to let themselves be found in this temptation, and then the kingdom is assured to them. It is the fundamental word of Jesus to all his disciples. 'But ye are they which have continued with me in my temptations, and I appoint unto you a kingdom' (Luke 22.28f.). It is not the temptations of the *disciples* which here receive the promise, but their participation in the life and the temptation of Jesus. The temptations of the disciples fall on *Jesus*, and the temptations of Jesus come upon the disciples. But to share in the atonement of Christ means to share also in Christ's overcoming and victory. It does not mean that the temptations of Christ had finished and that the disciples would no longer suffer them. They will indeed suffer temptations, but it will be the temptations of Jesus Christ which befall them. Christ has also won the victory over these temptations.

It is by the disciples sharing in the temptation of Jesus Christ that Jesus will protect his disciples from other temptation: 'Watch and pray, that ye enter not into temptation' (Matt. 26.41). What temptation threatened the disciples in the hour of Gethsemane, if it was not that they should be offended at the passion of Christ, and they would not share in his temptations? So Jesus uses here the petition of the Lord's Prayer: 'Lead us not into temptation'. Finally, it is the same thing when it says in Hebrews 2.18: 'For in that he himself hath suffered being tempted, he is able to succour them that are tempted'. This is not only a question of the help which he alone can give who has learnt to know the need and suffering of the other man in his own experience. The true meaning is rather that in my temptations my real succour is only in his temptation; to share in his temptation is the only help in my temptation. Thus I ought not to think of my temptation other than as the temptation of Jesus Christ. In his temptation is my succour; for here only is victory and overcoming.

The practical task of the Christian must, therefore, be to understand all the temptations which come upon him as temptations of Jesus Christ in him, and thus he will be aided. But how does it happen? Before we can speak of the concrete temptations of Christians and their overcoming, the question of the author of the temptation of Christians must be put. Only when the Christian knows with whom he has to do in temptation, can he act rightly in the actual event.

The Three Authors of Temptation

The Holy Scriptures call the different authors of the temptation: the devil, the lust of man, God himself.

The Devil

What does the Bible say when it calls the devil the author of temptation? It says, first, that temptation is entirely against God. It is inconceivable, from the character of God, that men should be tempted by God to doubt in God's Word and to apostasy. The tempter is always the enemy of God. Secondly, the enemy of God shows in temptation his power to do something that is not the will of God. What no creature could do for himself, that the wicked enemy can do, that is to say that the temptation is a *power* which is stronger than any creature. It is the invasion of Satan's power into the world of creation. If the devil is the tempter, no creature can withstand temptation in his own strength. He must fall. So great is the power of Satan (Eph. 6.12). Thirdly, the temptation is seduction, leading astray. Therefore it is of the devil; for the devil is a liar. 'When he speaketh a lie, he speaketh of his own: for he is a liar, and the father thereof' (John 8.44). Sin is a deceit (Heb. 3.13). The deceit, the lie of the devil consists of this, that he wishes to make man believe that he can live without God's Word. Thus he dangles before man's phantasy a kingdom of faith, of power and of peace, into which only he can enter who consents to the temptations; and he conceals from men that he, as the devil, is the most unfortunate and unhappy of beings, since he is finally and eternally rejected by God. Fourthly, temptation comes from the devil; for here the devil becomes the accuser of man. There are two parts to every temptation: man must be alienated from the Word of God, and God must be forced to reject man, because the accuser has exposed his sins. About this second part we can say this. Job's is the prototype of all temptations. Satan's question is: 'Doth Job fear God for nought? Hast not thou made an hedge about him, and about his house, and about all that he hath, on every side? Thou hast blessed the work of his hands, and his substance is increased in the land. But put forth thine hand now, and touch all that he hath, and will he not renounce thee to thy face?' (Job 1.9ff.). Here the meaning of all temptation is clear. Everything that a man has is taken from him, and he is in the end made completely powerless. Poverty, sickness, scorn and rejection by the pious plunge him into darkest night. Everything of which Satan as prince of this world can rob man he takes from him. He drives him into the loneliness in which for the tempted nothing remains but God. And even here it must be made known that man does not fear God for nought, that he does not love God for God's sake but for the sake of the good things of this world. At some place Satan will make it clear that Job does not fear God, love and trust him, above all things. Thus every temptation is a revelation of sin, and the accuser stands there more righteous than God; for he has uncovered sin. He compels God to judge.

So the devil shows himself in temptation as the enemy of God, as power, as a liar and as accuser. For men in temptation it means this: that the enemy of God must be recognized in temptation; that the power which is opposed to God must be overcome in temptation; that the lie must be unmasked in temptation.

As to how this can actually be accomplished, more later. We must ask further questions.

Lust

What does the Bible say about the lust of men as the author of their temptation? 'Let no man say when he is tempted, I am tempted of God: for God cannot be tempted with evil, and he himself tempteth no man: but each man is tempted, when he is drawn away by his own lust, and enticed. Then the lust, when it hath conceived, beareth sin: and the sin, when it is fullgrown, bringeth forth death' (James 1.31ff.).

First, he who transfers the guilt of the temptation to someone other than himself, thereby justifies his fall. If I am not guilty in my temptation, neither am I guilty when I perish in it. Temptation is guilt in so far as the fall is inexcusable. It is therefore impossible to put the guilt of temptation on to the devil; then all the more is it a blasphemy to make God answerable for it. It may appear pious, but in truth the statement implies that God is himself in some way open to evil. This would attribute division to God, which makes his Word and his will questionable, ambiguous, doubtful. Since evil has no place in God, not even the possibility of evil, temptation to evil must never be laid at God's door. God himself tempts no one. The source of temptation lies in my own self. Secondly, temptation is punishment. The place in which all temptation originates is my evil desires. My own longing for pleasure, and my fear of suffering, entice me to let go the Word of God. The hereditary depraved nature of the flesh is the source of the evil inclinations of body and soul, as are men and things, which now become temptation. Neither the beauty of the world, nor suffering, are in themselves evil and tempting, but our evil desires which win pleasure from all this and which let themselves be suborned and enticed, turn all this into temptation for us. While in the devilish origin of temptation the objectivity of temptation must become clear, here its complete subjectivity is emphasized. Both are equally necessary.

Thirdly, desire in itself does not make me sinful. But 'when it hath conceived, it beareth sin, and the sin, when it is fullgrown, bringeth forth death.' Desire conceives by the union of my 'I' with it—when I abandon the Word of God which upholds me. As long as desire remains untouched by my self, it is an 'It'. But sin occurs only through the 'I'. Thus the source of temptation lies in the ἐπιθυμία, the source of sin is in my self, and in my self alone. Therefore I must acknowledge that mine alone is the guilt and that I deserve eternal death when in temptation I succumb to sin. Jesus indeed pronounces a terrible judgement on him who tempts the innocent, who offends one of the little ones; 'Woe unto him who tempts another to sin'—that is what the Word of God says about every tempter. But yours alone is the guilt in your sin and your death, if you submit to the temptation of your desire. That is God's Word to the tempted.

God himself

What does the Bible say about God when it makes him the author of temptation? That is the most difficult and final question. God tempts no one, says James. But the Bible also says that 'God did prove Abraham'

(Gen. 22.1), that Israel was tempted by God (II Chron. 32.31). David at the census was 'made angry by the wrath of God' (II Sam. 24.1), 'by Satan'—according to I Chron. 21.1). Likewise in the New Testament the temptation of Christians is looked upon as the judgement of God (I Pet. 4.12, 17). What does it all mean?

First, the Bible makes it clear that nothing can happen on earth without the will and permission of God. Satan also is in God's hands. He must—against his will—serve God. It is true that Satan has power, but only where God allows it to him. There is consolation for the tempted believer. Satan had to ask permission from God for Job's temptation. He can do nothing on his own. Thus God must first abandon man in order that Satan may have opportunity for temptation—'God left Hezekiah to try him' (II Chron. 32.31). This is how we should understand everything that was said earlier about the abandonment of the tempted. God gives the tempted into Satan's hands.

Second—the child's question: 'Why doesn't God simply strike Satan dead?' demands an answer. We know that the same question can mean: Why must Christ be tempted, suffer and die? Why must Satan have such power over him? God gives Satan opportunity because of men's sin. Satan must execute the death of the sinner; for only if the sinner dies, can the righteous man live; only if the old man daily and wholly perishes, can the new man rise from the dead. While Satan thus employs himself, he serves God's purpose. 'The Lord killeth, and maketh alive: He bringeth down to the grave, and bringeth up' (I Sam. 2.6). So must Satan unwillingly serve God's plan of redemption; with Satan rests death and sin, but with God life and righteousness. Satan does his work in three ways in temptation. He leads men to the knowledge of sin. He allows the flesh to suffer. He gives death to the sinner.

1. 'God left him, to try him, that he might know all that was in his heart' (II Chron. 32.31). The heart of man is revealed in temptation. Man knows his sin, which without temptation he could never have known; for in temptation man knows on what he has set his heart. The coming to light of sin is the work of the accuser, who thereby thinks to have won the victory. But it is sin which is become manifest which can be known and therefore forgiven. Thus the manifestation of sin belongs to the salvation plan of God with man, and Satan must serve this plan.

2. In temptation Satan wins power over the believer as far as he is flesh. He torments him by enticement to lust, by the pains of privation, and by bodily and spiritual suffering of every kind. He robs him of everything he has and, at the same time, entices him to forbidden happiness. He drives him, like Job, into the abyss, into the darkness, in which the tempted one is only sustained by the grace of God which he does not perceive and feel, but which nevertheless holds him fast. So Satan appears to have won full power over the believer, but this victory turns to complete defeat. For the mortification of the flesh is indeed the way to life in judgement; and the tempted one, in being driven into a complete void and into defencelessness, is driven by Satan directly into the very hands of God. Thus Christ recognizes at once in Satan's fury the gracious chastening of God (Heb. 12.4ff.), of the Father to his child; the gracious judgement of God which preserves man from the judgement of wrath. The hour of temptation, therefore, becomes the hour of greatest joy (James 1.2ff.).

3. The last enemy is death. Death is in Satan's hands. The sinner dies. Death is the last temptation. But even here where man loses everything, where hell reveals its terror, even here life has broken in upon the believer. Satan loses his last power and his last right over the

believer. We ask once more: Why does God give Satan opportunity for temptation? First, in order finally to overcome Satan. Through getting his rights Satan is destroyed. As God punishes the godless man by allowing him to be godless, and allowing him his right and his freedom, and as the godless man perishes in this freedom of his (Rom. 1.19ff.), so God does not destroy Satan by an act of violence, but Satan must destroy himself. Second, God gives opportunity to Satan in order to bring believers to salvation. Only by knowledge of sin, by suffering and death, can the new man live. Third, the overcoming of Satan and the salvation of believers is true and real in Jesus Christ alone. Satan plagues Jesus with all sins, all suffering and the death of mankind. But with that his power is at an end. He had taken everything from Jesus Christ and thereby delivered him to God alone. Thus we are led to the knowledge from which we set out: Believers must learn to understand all their temptations as the temptation of Jesus Christ in them. In this way they will share in the victory.

But how can the Bible say that God tempts man? It speaks of the wrath of God, of which Satan is the executor (cf. II Sam. 24.1; I Chron. 21.1). The wrath of God lay upon Jesus Christ from the hour of the temptation. It struck Jesus because of the sin of the flesh which he wore. And because the wrath of God found obedience, for the sake of sin, obedience even unto the righteous death of him who bore the sin of the whole world, the wrath was propitiated, the wrath of God had driven Jesus to the gracious God, the grace of God had overcome the wrath of God, the power of Satan was conquered. But where the whole temptation of the flesh, all the wrath of God is obediently endured in Jesus Christ, there the temptation is conquered in Jesus Christ, there the Christian finds behind the God of wrath who tempts him the God of grace who tempts no one.

IV

CONCRETE TEMPTATIONS AND THEIR CONQUEST

IN the concrete temptation of Christ there is also, therefore, to be distinguished the hand of the devil and the hand of God, there is the question of resistance and of submission in the right place; that is, resistance to the devil is only possible in the fullest submission to the hand of God.

This must now be made clear in detail. Since all temptations of believers are temptations of Christ in his members, of the body of Christ, we speak of these temptations in the analogy of the temptation of Christ. (1) Of fleshly temptation. (2) Of high spiritual temptations. (3) Of the last temptation. But I Cor. 10.12ff. is true of all temptations: 'Wherefore let him that thinketh he standeth take heed lest he fall. There hath no temptation taken you but such as man can bear: but God is faithful, who will not suffer you to be tempted above that ye are able; but will with the temptation make also the way of escape, that ye may be able to endure it.' Here St. Paul opposes first all false security and, secondly, all false despondency in face of temptation. No one can be sure even for a moment that he can remain free from temptation. There is no temptation which could not attack me suddenly at this moment. No one can think that Satan is far from him. 'Be sober, be watchful: your adversary the devil, as a roaring lion, walketh about, seeking whom he may devour.' (I Pet.

5.8). Not for one moment in this life are we secure from temptation and fall. Therefore do not be proud if you see another stumble and fall. Such security will be a snare for you. 'Be not high-minded, but fear' (Rom. 11.20). Rather be at all time ready that the tempter find no power in you.

'Watch and pray, that ye enter not into temptation' (Matt. 26.41). Be on your guard against the crafty enemy, pray to God that he hold us fast in his Word and his grace—that is the attitude of the Christian towards temptation.

But the Christian must not be afraid of temptation. If it comes upon him in spite of watching and praying, then he should know that he can conquer every temptation. There is no temptation which cannot be conquered. God knows our abilities, and he will not let us be tempted beyond our power. It is *human* temptation which harasses us, that is to say, it is not too big for us men. God allots to every man that portion which he can bear. That is certain. He who loses courage because of the suddenness and the awfulness of temptation, has forgotten the main point, namely that he will quite certainly withstand the temptation because God will not let it go beyond that which he is able to endure. There are temptations by which we are particularly frightened because we are so often wrecked upon them. When they are suddenly there again, we so often give ourselves up for lost from the beginning. But we must look at these temptations in the greatest peace and composure for they can be conquered, and they are conquered, so certain is it that God is faithful. Temptation must find us in humility and in certainty of victory.

The Temptations of the Flesh

We speak first of temptation by desire and then of temptation by suffering.

Desire

In our members there is a slumbering inclination towards desire which is both sudden and fierce. With irresistible power desire seizes mastery over the flesh. All at once a secret, smouldering fire is kindled. The flesh burns and is in flames. It makes no difference whether it is sexual desire, or ambition, or vanity, or desire for revenge, or love of fame and power, or greed for money, or, finally, that strange desire for the beauty of the world, of nature. Joy in God is in course of being extinguished in us and we seek all our joy in the creature. At this moment God is quite unreal to us, he loses all reality, and only desire for the creature is real; the only reality is the devil. Satan does not here fill us with hatred of God, but with forgetfulness of God. And now his falsehood is added to this proof of strength. The lust thus aroused envelops the mind and will of man in deepest darkness. The powers of clear discrimination and of decision are taken from us. The questions present themselves: 'Is what the flesh desires really sin in this case?' 'Is it really not permitted to me, yes—expected of me, now, here, in my particular situation, to appease desire?' The tempter puts me in a privileged position as he tried to put the hungry Son of God in a privileged position. I boast of my privilege against God.

It is here that everything within me rises up against the Word of God. Powers of the body, the mind and the will, which were held in obedience under the discipline of the Word, of which I believed that I was the master, make it clear to me that I am by no means master of them. 'All my powers forsake me', laments the psalmist.

They have all gone over to the adversary. The adversary deploys my powers against me. In this situation I can no longer act as a hero; I am a defenceless, powerless man. God himself has forsaken me. Who can conquer, who can gain the victory?

None other than the Crucified, Jesus Christ himself, for whose sake all this happens to me; for he is by me and in me, and therefore temptation besets me as it beset him.

There is only one stronger reality to be set against the exclusive reality of desire and of Satan: the image and the presence of the Crucified. Against this power the power of desire breaks up into nothingness; for here it is conquered. Here the flesh has received its right and its reward, namely death. Here I realize that the lust of the flesh is nothing else than the anguish of the flesh in the face of death. Because Christ is the death of the flesh, and because this Christ is within me, the dying flesh rears itself up against Christ. Now I know that the death of the flesh is manifested in the temptation of the flesh. The flesh dies because it kindles lust and desire. In the temptation of the flesh I share in the death of Jesus in the flesh. So the temptation of the flesh which draws me into the death of the flesh, drives me into the death of Christ, who died in the flesh but who is raised in the spirit. Only the death of Christ rescues me from the temptation of the flesh.

Therefore the Bible teaches us in times of temptation in the flesh to *flee*: 'Flee fornication' (I Cor. 6.18)—'from idolatry' (I Cor. 10.14)—'youthful lusts' (II Tim. 2.22)—'the lust of the world' (II Pet. 1.4). There is no resistance to Satan other than flight. Every struggle against lust in one's own strength is doomed to failure. Flee—that can indeed only mean, Flee to that place where you find protection and help, flee to the Crucified. His image and his presence alone can help. Here we see the crucified body and perceive in it the end of all desire; here we see right through Satan's deceit and here our spirit again becomes sober and aware of the enemy. Here I perceive the forsakenness and abandonment of my fleshly condition and the righteous judgement of God's wrath on all flesh. Here I know that in this lost condition I could never have helped myself against Satan, but that it is the victory of Jesus Christ which I now share. But here also I find ground for the attitude in which alone I can conquer all temptations—for patience (James 1.2ff.). I ought not to rebel against the temptations of the flesh in unlawful pride, as though I were too good for them. I ought to and I can humble myself under the hand of God and endure patiently the humiliation of such temptations. So I discern in the midst of Satan's deadly work the righteous and merciful punishment of God. In the death of Jesus I find refuge from Satan and the communion of death in the flesh under temptation and of life in the spirit through his victory.

Suffering

This makes it clear that temptation by desire means to the Christian not desire but suffering. Temptation to desire always includes the renunciation of the desire, that is to say, suffering. Temptation to suffering always includes the longing for freedom from suffering, that is to say, for desire. Thus temptation of the flesh through desire and through suffering is at bottom one and the same.

We shall speak first of the temptation of the Christian through general sufferings, that is through sickness, poverty, need of all kinds; after that, of the temptation of the Christian through suffering for the sake of Christ.

General Suffering. If the Christian should fall into serious sickness, bitter poverty or other severe suffering, he should know that the devil has his hand in the game. Stoical resignation, which accepts everything as inevitable, is a self-defence of the man who will not acknowledge the devil and God. It has nothing to do with faith in God. The Christian knows that suffering in this world is linked with the fall of man, and that God does not will sickness, suffering and death. The Christian perceives in suffering a temptation of Satan to separate him from God. It is here that murmuring against God has its origin. While God disappears from man's sight in the fire of lust, the heat of affliction easily leads him into conflict with God. The Christian threatens to doubt the love of God. Why does God allow this suffering? God's justice is incomprehensible to him. Why must it happen to me? What have I done to deserve it? By suffering God should become our joy. Job is the Biblical prototype of this temptation. Everything is taken from Job by Satan, in order that in the end he may curse God. Violent pain, hunger and thirst can rob man of all his strength and lead him to the edge of apostasy.

How does the Christian conquer the temptation of suffering? Here the end of the Book of Job is a great help to us. In the face of suffering Job has protested his innocence to the last, and has brushed aside the counsels to repentance from his friends who try to trace his misfortune back to a particular, perhaps hidden sin of Job. In addition, Job has spoken high-sounding words about his own righteousness. After the appearance of God Job declares: 'Therefore have I uttered that which I understood not . . . . wherefore I abhor myself, and repent in dust and ashes' (Job 42.3, 6). But the wrath of God is not now turned against Job, but against his friends: 'for ye have not spoken of me the thing that is right, as my servant Job hath' (Job 42.7). Job gets justice before God and yet confesses his guilt before God. That is the

CONCRETE TEMPTATIONS

solution of the problem. Job's suffering has its foundation not in his guilt but in his righteousness. Job is tempted because of his piety. So Job is right to protest against suffering coming upon him as if he were guilty. Yet this right comes to an end for Job when he no longer faces man but faces God. Face to face with God, even the good, innocent Job knows himself to be guilty.

This means for the Christian, tempted by suffering, that he must and should protest against suffering in so far as, in doing so, he protests against the devil and asserts his own innocence. The devil has broken into God's order and is the cause of suffering (Luther on Lenchen's death!). But in the presence of God the Christian also sees his sufferings as judgement on the sin of all flesh, which also dwells in his own flesh. He recognizes his sin and confesses himself to be guilty. 'Thine own wickedness shall correct thee, and thy backslidings shall reprove thee. Know therefore and see that it is an evil thing and a bitter, that thou hast forsaken the Lord thy God, and that my fear is not in thee, saith the Lord, the Lord of hosts' (Jer. 2.19; 4.18). Suffering, therefore, leads to the knowledge of sin, and thereby, to the return to God. We see our suffering as the judgement of God on our flesh, and because of that we can be grateful for it. For judgement on the flesh, the death of the old man is only the side turned towards the world of the life of the new man. Thus it is said: 'He that hath suffered in the flesh hath ceased from sin' (I Pet. 4.1). All suffering must lead the Christian to the strengthening of his faith and not to defection. While the flesh shuns suffering and rejects it, the Christian sees his suffering as the suffering of Christ in him. For he has borne our griefs and carried our sorrows. He bore God's wrath on sin. He died in the flesh, and so we also die in the flesh, because he lives in us.

Now the Christian understands his suffering, also, as the temptation of Christ in him. That leads him into patience, into the silent, waiting endurance of temptation, and fills him with gratitude; for the more the old man dies, the more certainly lives the new man; the deeper man is driven into suffering, the nearer he comes to Christ. Just because Satan took everything from Job, he cast him on God alone. So for the Christian suffering becomes a protest against the devil, a recognition of his own sin, the righteous judgement of God, the death of his old man, and communion with Jesus Christ.

Suffering for Christ's Sake. Whereas the Christian must endure the sufferings of this world, just like the godless, there is reserved for the Christian a suffering of which the world knows nothing: suffering for the sake of the Lord Jesus Christ (I Pet. 4.12, 17). This suffering, too, happens to him as temptation (πρὸς πειρασμόν, I Pet. 4.12; cf. Judg. 2.22). While the Christian can understand all general sufferings as consequences of the general sin of the flesh, in which he too shares, the fact of his suffering on account of his righteousness, on account of his faith, must indeed seem strange to him. That the righteous man suffers on account of his sin is understandable; but that the righteous man suffers for the sake of righteousness, that can easily lead him to the stumbling-block in Jesus Christ. Temptation here is so much the greater than in the suffering which is common to all (sickness, poverty, etc.), which cannot be avoided, because this suffering for Christ's sake would end immediately with the denial of Christ. It is therefore to some extent voluntary suffering from which I can escape again. And just here Satan has a free field of operation. He stirs up the longing of the flesh for happiness, he makes the good insights of the Christian take up arms against him, so that he can show the Christian the folly and the wickedness of his voluntary suffering, the pious way out, the special solution of his conflict. Unavoidable suffering is indeed a severe temptation; but much heavier is the suffering which, in the opinion of the world and of my flesh and even of my pious thoughts, is avoidable. The freedom of man is deployed against the bondage of the Christian.

That is a real temptation to apostasy. But the Christian will not be surprised by this temptation; he ought rather to understand that he is here led right into the communion of the sufferings of Christ (I Pet. 4.13). The temptation of the devil drives the Christian afresh into the arms of Jesus Christ, the crucified. At the very point where Satan robs man of his freedom and sets him against Christ, there is the bondage of the Christian in Jesus Christ most gloriously visible. What do we mean when we speak of sharing in the sufferings of Christ? It means first joy (χαίρετε, I Pet. 4.13). It means awareness of innocence where the Christian suffers 'as a Christian' (ὡς χριστιανός, I Pet. 4.16). It means a glorifying of God in the name of Christian, which I bear (δοξαζέτω, I Pet. 4.16). The Christian suffers 'in the behalf of Christ' (Phil. 1.29). But, finally and essentially, it means the understanding of the judgement which begins at the house of God (I Pet. 4.17). This is a hard thought—that the suffering which I suffer as a Christian, as a righteous man, can also be understood as a judgement upon sin; and simply everything lies in the combination of these two bits of knowledge. A suffering for Christ's sake which acknowledges no element of judgement in it is fanaticism. What kind of a judgement are we thinking of? The *one* judgement of God which came upon Christ and will come upon all flesh in the end—the judgement of God on sin. No man can give himself to Christ without sharing in this judgement of God. For it is that which distinguishes Christ from the world, that he bore the judgement which the world despised and rejected. The difference is not that judgement came not upon Christ but upon the world; it is rather that Christ, the sinless one, bore God's judgement on sin. So to 'belong to Christ' means to bow oneself beneath the judgement of God. It is that which distinguishes suffering in the fellowship of Jesus Christ from suffering in the fellowship of any other ethical or political hero. In suffering the Christian recognizes guilt and judgement. What guilt is it over which he recognizes judgement? It is the guilt of all flesh, which the Christian, too, bears until his life's end; but, beyond that, it is at the same time the guilt of the world in Jesus, which falls upon him and which allows him to suffer. Thus his righteous suffering in the fellowship of Jesus Christ becomes vicarious suffering for the world.

But since Christ himself submitted to the judgement of God, he is taken out of the judgement (Isa. 53.8), and because Christians now bow themselves beneath the judgement, they are saved from the wrath and judgement to come. 'And if the righteous is scarcely saved' (that is, from the temptation which comes upon him in this suffering), 'where shall the ungodly and sinner appear?' (I Pet. 4.18). As judgement at the house of God is a judgement of grace on Christians, so the final judgement of wrath must fall upon the godless.

So the Christian recognizes in his suffering for the sake of Jesus Christ, first, the devil, and his temptation to fall from Christ; second, the joy, to be allowed to suffer for Christ; third, the judgement of God at the house of God. He knows that he suffers 'according to the will of God' (I Pet. 4.19) and, in the fellowship of the cross, he grasps the grace of God.

The Temptations of the Spirit

Jesus repelled the second temptation of Satan with the words 'Thou shalt not tempt the Lord thy God'. Satan had tempted Jesus to ask for a visible acknowledgement of his divine Sonship, not to let himself be satisfied with God's Word and promise, and to want more than faith. Jesus called such a demand tempting God, that is, the putting to the proof of the faithfulness of God, the truth of God, the love of God, and attributing to God faithlessness, falsehood and lack of love, instead of looking for them in oneself. All temptation which aims directly at our faith in salvation brings us into the danger of tempting God.

The temptations of the spirit, therefore, with which the devil tempts Christians, have a double aim. The believer is to fall into the sin of spiritual pride (*securitas*) or perish in the sin of despair (*desperatio*). But in both sins there is the one sin of tempting God.

Securitas

The devil tempts us in the sin of spiritual pride, in that he deceives us about the seriousness of God's law and of God's wrath. He takes the word of God's grace in his hand and whispers to us, God is a God of grace, he will not take our sins so seriously. So he awakens in us the longing to sin against God's grace and to assign forgiveness to ourselves even before our sin. He makes us secure in grace. We are God's children, we have Christ and his cross, we are the true church, no evil can now befall us. God will no longer hold us responsible for our sin. What spells ruin for others has no longer any danger for us. Through grace we have a privileged position before God. Here wanton sin threatens grace (Jude 4). Here it says: 'Where is the God of judgement?' (Mal. 2.17), and 'we call the proud happy; yea, they that work wickedness are built up; yea, they tempt God, and are delivered' (Mal. 3.15). From such talk follows all indolence of the spirit in prayer and in obedience, indifference to the Word of God, the deadening of conscience, the contempt of the good conscience, 'shipwreck concerning the faith' (I Tim. 1.19). (Man persists in unforgiven sin and daily piles up guilt upon guilt.) Lastly there follows the complete hardening and obduracy of the heart in sin, in fearlessness and security before God, hypocritical piety (Acts 5.3 and 9!). There is no longer any room for repentance, man can no longer obey. This way ends in idolatry. The God of grace has now become an idol which I serve. This is clearly the tempting of God which provokes the wrath of God.

Spiritual pride arises from disregard of the law and of the wrath of God; whether I say that I am able to stand in my own goodness according to the law of God (justification by works); or whether I, through grace, bestow upon myself a privilege to sin (Nomism and Antinomianism). God is tempted in both, because I put to the test the seriousness of his wrath and demand a sign beyond his Word.

Desperatio

The temptation to *desperatio*, to despair (*acedia*) corresponds to the temptation to *securitas*. Here not the law and the wrath, but the grace and promise of God are attacked and put to the test. In this way Satan robs the believer of all joy in the Word of God, all experience of the good God; in place of which he fills the heart with the terrors of the past, of the present and of the future. Old long-forgotten guilt suddenly rears up its head before me, as if it had happened today. Opposition to the Word of God and unwillingness to obey assume huge proportions, and complete despair of my future before God overwhelms my heart. God was never with me, God is not with me, God will never forgive me; for my sin is so great that it cannot be forgiven. Thus man's spirit is in rebellion against the Word of God. Man now demands an experience, proof of the grace of God. Otherwise, in his despair of God he will no longer listen to his Word. And this despair drives him either into the sin of blasphemy or into self-destruction, to the extremity of despair, to suicide, like Saul and Judas; or man, in despair of God's grace, will try to create for himself the sign that God refuses him; in his own strength he will be a saint—in defiance of God—in self-annihilating asceticism and works—or even by magic.

In ingratitude, in disobedience, and in hopelessness, man hardens himself against the grace of God. Satan demands a sign that he is a saint. The promise of God in Christ is no longer sufficient. 'And that is the hardest and highest temptation and suffering, that God sometimes attacks and exercises his greatest saints—which man is in the habit of calling *desertio gratiae*, when the heart of man feels nothing less than that God has abandoned him with his grace, and he no longer wishes to live'. 'But it is difficult for the human heart to accept consolation, for when our Lord God heartens a man, his soul wishes to depart from him, his eyes swim with tears and the sweat of fear breaks out.' (Luther on Gen. 35.1.)

When Satan deploys God's Word in the law against God's Word in Christ, when he becomes the accuser who allows man to find no comfort, then we ought to think of the following: First, it is the devil himself who here puts God's Word into the mouth. Second, we should never argue with the devil about our sins, but we should speak about our sins only with Jesus. Third, we should tell the devil that Jesus has called to himself not the righteous but sinners, and that we—in defiance of the devil—wish to remain sinners in order to be with Jesus rather than be righteous with the devil. Fourth, we should understand how, in such temptation, our own sin is punished by the wrath of God and comes to light; that is, first, our ingratitude in face of everything that God has done for us up to this moment. 'Forget not what good he has done you'. 'Whoso offereth the sacrifice of thanksgiving glorifieth me, and to him ... will I shew the salvation of God' (Ps. 50.23); second, our present disobedience which will do no penance for unforgiven sin and will not relinquish its favourite sin (For unforgiven, cherished sin is the best gateway by which the devil can invade our hearts); and, finally, our hopelessness, as though our sins were too great for God, as though Christ had suffered only for trivial sins and not for the real and great sins of the whole world, as though God did not still purpose great things even with me, as though he had not prepared an inheritance in heaven even for me. Fifth, I ought to thank God for his judgement on me, which shows me that he 'heartens' and loves me. Sixth, I must recognize in all this that I am here thrust by Satan into the highest temptation of Christ on the cross, as he cried: 'My God, my God, why hast thou forsaken me'. But where God's wrath broke out, there was reconciliation. Where I, smitten by God's wrath, lose everything, there I hear the words: 'My grace is sufficient for thee; for my power is made perfect in weakness' (II Cor. 12.9). Lastly, in gratitude for temptation overcome I know, at the same time, that no temptation is more terrible than to be without temptation.

The Last Temptation

As to how Satan repeats the third temptation of Jesus on believers there is not much to be said. Here it is a matter of the unconcealed appearance of Satan, in which he tempts us to a wilful and final defection from God, by promising us, through the worship of Satan, all power and all happiness on this earth. Just as temptations of the spirit are not experienced by all Christians, since they would go beyond their powers, so this last temptation certainly comes only to a very few men. Christ has suffered it and conquered; and who would dare to say that Antichrist and the ἀντι-χριστοί must have suffered this temptation and have fallen. Where there is a wilful alliance with Satan through spirit or through blood, there the power has broken in which the Bible describes as wanton sin, for which there is no forgiveness, which tramples underfoot the Son of God, which crucifies the Son of God afresh, the abuse of the Spirit of grace (Heb. 10.26 and 6.6), the sin unto death, for which a man ought no longer to pray (I John 5.16ff.), the sin against the Holy Ghost, for which there is no forgiveness (Matt. 12.31ff.). He who has experienced this temptation and has conquered, has indeed won the victory over all temptations.

V

THE LEGITIMATE STRUGGLE

ALL temptation is temptation of Jesus Christ and all victory is victory of Jesus Christ. All temptation leads the believer into the deepest solitude, into abandonment by men and by God. But in this solitude he finds Jesus Christ, man and God. The blood of Christ and the example of Christ and the prayer of Christ are his help and his strength. The Book of Revelation says of the redeemed: 'They overcame . . . because of the blood of the lamb' (Rev. 12.11). Not by the spirit, but by the blood of Christ is the devil overcome. Therefore in all temptation we must get back to this blood, in which is all our help. Then, too, there is the image of Jesus Christ which we should look upon in the hour of temptation. 'See the end of the Lord' (James 5.11). His patience in suffering is the death of the flesh, the suffering of our flesh is made to seem of small account, we are preserved from all pride and comforted in all sorrow. The prayer of Jesus Christ which he promised to Peter: 'Simon, behold, Satan asked to have you, that he might sift you as wheat, but I made supplication for thee' (Luke 22.31) represents our weak prayer before the Father in heaven, who does not allow us to be tempted beyond our powers.

Believers suffer the hour of temptation without defence. Jesus Christ is their shield. And only when it is quite clearly understood that temptation must befall the Godforsaken, then the word can at last be uttered which the Bible speaks about the Christian's struggle. From heaven the Lord gives to the defenceless the heavenly armour before which, though men's eyes do not see it, Satan flees. *He* clothes us with the armour of God, *he* gives into our hand the shield of faith, *he* sets upon our brow the helmet of salvation, *he* gives us the sword of the spirit in the right hand. It is the garment of Christ, the robe of his victory, that he puts upon his struggling community.

The Spirit teaches us that the time of temptations is not yet ended, but that the hardest temptation is still to come to his people. But he promises also: 'Because thou didst keep the word of my patience, I also will keep thee from the hour of trial, that hour which is to come upon the whole world, to try them that dwell upon the earth. I come quickly' (Rev. 3.10ff.), and 'The Lord knoweth how to deliver the godly out of temptation' (II Pet. 2.9).

So we pray, as Jesus Christ has taught us, to the Father in heaven: 'Lead us not into temptation' and we know that our prayer is heard, for all temptation is conquered in Jesus Christ for all time, unto the end. So together with James we say: 'Blessed is the man that endureth temptation, for when he hath been approved, he shall receive the crown of life, which the Lord promised to them that love him' (James 1.12). The promise of Jesus Christ proclaims: 'Ye are they which have continued with me in my temptations, and I appoint unto you a kingdom' (Luke 22.28f.).

CPSIA information can be obtained
at www.ICGtesting.com
Printed in the USA
BVHW050355300123
657341BV00022B/306

9 780334 051602